RUIN YOUR LIFE

An Invitation to Let God Re-create the Real You

AUTHOR : _____
your name here

RU↓N
YOUR
LIFE

An Invitation to
let God Re-create
the Real you

CHRIS FOLMSBEE & NATE SEVERSON

ZONDERVAN

Ruin Your Life
Copyright © 2011 by Chris Folmsbee and Nate Severson

YS Youth Specialties is a trademark of Real Resources Incorporated and is registered with the United States Patent and Trademark Office.

This title is also available as a Zondervan ebook.

Requests for information should be addressed to:

Zondervan, 3900 *Sparks Dr. SE, Grand Rapids, Michigan 49546*

Library of Congress Cataloging-in-Publication Data

Folmsbee, Chris.
     Ruin your life : an invitation to let God re-create the real you / by Chris Folmsbee.
        p. cm
     ISBN 978-0-310-32562-8 (softcover)
     1. Christian teenagers—Religious life—Miscellanea. I. Title. II. Title: Invitation to let God re-create the real you.
     BV4531.3.F655   2010
     248.8´3—dc23

                                             2011044326

Cover design: SharpSeven Design
Interior design: David Conn and Ben Fetterley

Printed in the United States of America

CONTENTS

HOW TO USE RUIN YOUR LIFE

You and your ideas matter a great deal. What you have to say to this world is very much needed. So we have created a book to help you say it first experimentally in a fun way so that later you can say it confidently for those you want to share it with. *Ruin Your Life* is our way to give you permission to take some risks in this earthly journey and get clear on what you're about.

Ruin Your Life is a fun process combining journaling, sketching, and scrapbooking. It features a fail-proof collection of activities and writing prompts, inviting you to record, create, and value the messiness that life often brings out.

It's a book series invented by two youth pastors with graphics by a young designer, all of whom know how to ruin their lives. This book encourages you to value your foolish, creative expressions as well: creating grass stains on a page, gluing on noodles, fingerprinting, collaging photos, etc. *Ruin Your Life* is a brand-new way of writing your first autobiography that only you can write! So with this book feel free to escape into the blank page by pouring out your life.

Ruin Your Life also can help you to behave like a little child again and discover what it is that fires you up, makes you laugh, or brings purpose and direction to your days. *Ruin Your Life* offers creative challenges, moments of comfort, and some deeper reflections as well. So have fun as you engage in this book, give generously to these pages and please give yourself permission to just *Ruin Your Life!*

EXPERIENCE:

Using an **unconventional tool**
and some **dirt** or **mud,**
mess up this **page.**

Then **trace** your **name**
in the **mess** you made.

REFLECT:

Consider all the **messy things** in your life.
How does God **call out** your name amid the **clutter?**

PRAYER:

Lord, thanks for not waiting for me to get it all together before showing me your love in the ultimate way.

VERSE:

"But God demonstrates his own love for us in this: While we were still sinners, Christ died for us." (Romans 5:8)

QUOTATION:

"Our life is full of brokenness—broken relationships, broken promises, broken expectations. How can we live with that brokenness without becoming bitter and resentful except by returning again and again to God's faithful presence in our lives."—Henri Nouwen

RULER

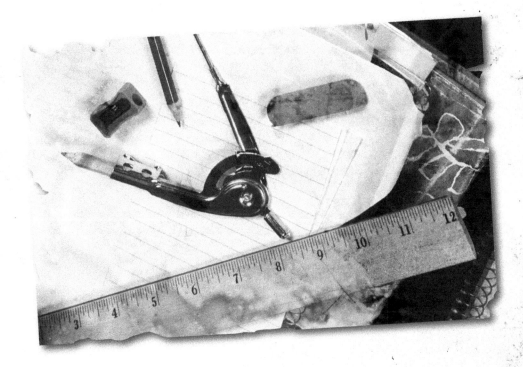

EXPERIENCE:

Draw **multiple boxes** on this page with a **ruler.** In the boxes, **write down** all the ways you **compare yourself** to others.

REFLECT:

Consider why it's wrong to try to "measure up" to others.

What attributes make you special?

PRAYER:

God, help me to become the person you want me to be.

VERSE:

"Am I now trying to win the approval of human beings, or of God? Or am I trying to please people? If I were still trying to please people, I would not be a servant of Christ." (Galatians 1:10)

QUOTATION:

"Define yourself radically as one beloved by God. This is the true self. Every other identity is illusion."

—Brennan Manning

CLOCK

EXPERIENCE:

Draw a clock
and label it
with all the things
that keep you busy
throughout the day.

REFLECT:

where do you see God in your busy day?

PRAYER:

Lord, help me to walk slowly enough to see you clearly in the midst of the blur called my life.

VERSE:

"I waited patiently for the LORD; he turned to me and heard my cry." (Psalm 40:1)

"But those who wait on the LORD shall renew their strength;
They shall mount up with wings like eagles,
They shall run and not be weary,
They shall walk and not faint." (Isaiah 40:31, NKJV)

"Be very careful, then, how you live—not as unwise but as wise, making the most of every opportunity, because the days are evil."
(Ephesians 5:15-16)

QUOTATION:

"People see God every day, they just don't recognize him."—Pearl Bailey

EXPERIENCE:

Drip the wax from a **burning candle** on this page.

Use a tool to write a **one-word prayer** in the wax before it dries.

How can you practice that prayer **daily?**

REFLECT:

It takes time for things to take shape.

What has God been forming in you lately?

PRAYER:

Lord, through the good and bad you continue to surprise me with the way you shape my life.

VERSE:

"Then the LORD God formed a man from the dust of the ground and breathed into his nostrils the breath of life..." (Genesis 2:7)

QUOTATION:

"Being a Christian is more than just an instantaneous conversion—it is a daily process whereby you grow to be more and more like Christ."—Billy Graham

FROST

EXPERIENCE:

Scrape some frost from the freezer walls and hold it in your hand.

Watch and feel it melt and write about what you're experiencing.

REFLECT:

What is it that can melt the frost in your life?

Who should you show more warmth and love to, and how do you plan on doing so?

PRAYER:

Lord, melt away the areas of my life that don't represent you and your unconditional love, and help me see your kindness as I share it with others.

VERSE:

"Be devoted to one another in love. Honor one another above yourselves."
(Romans 12:10)

QUOTATION:

"Be kind, for everyone you meet is fighting a hard battle."—Plato

IMPRINT

EXPERIENCE:

Place something with texture
under this page,
press down,
and color over the object
to reveal its form.

REFLECT:

Rubbing brings out the **true identity** of the "hidden" object.

What can people **learn** about you when they **get** to know your **true identity?**

What might you **be hiding?**

PRAYER:

Lord, I know **your imprint** is on me. Give me the **courage** to allow others to see my life in a real and **authentic** way.

VERSE:

"I can do **all this** through him who **gives me strength.**" (Philippians 4:13)

QUOTATION:

"**Committing yourself** is a way of finding out who you are. A man finds his **identity** by **identifying.**"—unknown

LOVE

(adoration, yearning, crush, devotion; expressing affection)

EXPERIENCE:

Think about the **people you love** the **most** and **write down** what you love **so much** about them.

REFLECT:

The love we express to others
is **directly related**
to the love we feel ourselves.

Do you believe this?
Why or why not?

PRAYER:

God, help me to believe that love is the greatest power in the world. Help me to see that love is not merely a feeling or sensation, but a vital attitude of life—an attitude of service for others in your name.

VERSE:

"Let love and faithfulness never leave you; bind them around your neck, write them on the tablet of your heart." (Proverbs 3:3)

QUOTATION:

"Love is, above all, the gift of oneself."
—Jean Anouilh

MIXTURE

EXPERIENCE:

Mix a few different **foods** from your kitchen in a bowl and **glue the labels** from those items here.

REFLECT:

What did you **notice** when you mixed the **substances together?**

Think about how many **good things** come from working with **others.**

PRAYER:

God, help me to **become more like Jesus** by taking on the **positive** characteristics of those who reflect and **collaborate** with him.

VERSE:

"**Two are better than one,** because they have a **good reward** for their toil. For if they fall, one will **lift up his fellow...**"
(Ecclesiastes 4:9-10a, ESV)

QUOTATION:

"**With collaboration** you never follow the same path twice."—anonymous

EXPERIENCE:

Cut
a few **strands** of your hair
and glue them here.

REFLECT:

Read the following verse:

"Indeed, the very hairs of your head
are all numbered.
Don't be afraid..."
(Luke 12:7a)

What are you worth?

How does it feel to know that
God knows every strand of hair
on your head
and pays attention to the
tiniest of details?

PRAYER:

Lord, words cannot do justice for the ways that you love and care for me.

FUN FACT:

The average human head has more than 100,000 hairs!

QUOTATION:

"My deepest awareness of myself is that I am deeply loved by Jesus Christ and I have done nothing to earn it or deserve it."

—Brennan Manning

MISTAKE
(error, misunderstanding, blooper)

EXPERIENCE:

Draw or describe your **most embarrassing** moment.

REFLECT:

What does it **feel like** to share your **most** embarrassing moment?

Read the following statement:
The **more you share** your most embarrassing moment, the **less embarrassing** it is.

Do you believe this? Why or why not?

PRAYER:

Lord, help me to develop the gift of humility so that I never become impressed with myself.

VERSE:

"The godly may trip seven times, but they will get up again..." (Proverbs 24:16, NLT)

QUOTATION:

"The only real mistake is the one from which we learn nothing."—John Powell

FEAR
(angst, anxiety, cold feet, doubt, nerves, worry)

EXPERIENCE:

Admit to what you're **most afraid of** and fill this page with words and images that represent **your fears.**

REFLECT:

What does it feel like
to admit your fears?

Read this statement: Learning to admit your fears allows you to treat them.

Do you agree? Why or why not?
(You are not alone in this.)

PRAYER/VERSE:

"When I am afraid, I put my trust in you. In God, whose word I praise—in God I trust and am not afraid. What can mere mortals do to me?" (Psalm 56:3-4)

QUOTATION:

"To the timid soul, nothing is possible."—John Bach

LISTEN
(accept, attend, lend an ear, tune in)

EXPERIENCE:

On a scale of 1-10,
how good a listener do you believe you are?

Ask a few others,
how good a listener
they believe you are.

REFLECT:

If the ratings differ, write down why.

How can you become a better listener?

PRAYER:

Lord, I have heard that I have **two ears** and **only one mouth** for a good reason. Help me to **double my listening ability** this day.

VERSE:

"My sheep **listen to my voice**; I know them, and **they follow me**." (John 10:27)

QUOTATION:

"You cannot **truly listen** to anyone and do **anything else** at the same time."—M. Scott Peck

WEAK
(powerless, wobbly, flimsy, frail, fragile)

EXPERIENCE:

Cut **photos** from a magazine that you believe **represent weakness.**

Glue them on this page and write down **why** you chose them.

REFLECT:

Who do you know
who's "weaker" than you?

What can you do to
extend your strength
to that person or those people?

PRAYER:

Lord, take what I have that is **weak in your eyes** and let it be a source of strength so others might **see your glory.**

VERSE:

"**Watch and pray** so that you **will not fall** into temptation. **The spirit is willing,** but the **flesh is weak.**" (Mark 14:38)

QUOTATION:

"The **awareness** of **our own strength** makes us **modest.**"—Paul Cezanne

FOOD

EXPERIENCE:

Give peanut butter and jelly sandwiches
to **someone in need.**

Smear some of the peanut butter and jelly
here to remind you about
what you can do to help
the many **hungry people** in the world.

Write about your experience.

BIG CHALLENGE:

Fast for the day.
What's it like to
go hungry for the day?
Write about that.

REFLECT:

How often are you hungry?
How do you suppose your hunger compares
to the **many people**
in the world living in **poverty**?

PRAYER:

God, help me to remember the hungry and resemble the Son of God. Remind me to share all that I have and help me to be grateful for all that I have.

VERSE:

Fasting reminds us that we are sustained "on every word that comes from the mouth of God." (Matthew 4:4)

QUOTATION:

"Food does not sustain us; God sustains us."
—Richard Foster

PHOTO

EXPERIENCE:

Find both an old and a recent
photograph of yourself
and glue them here.

PHOTO   67

REFLECT:

In what ways are you **different** now?

How have you **grown up spiritually** from **then** to now?

PRAYER:

I praise you, oh Lord, that you are the same yesterday, today, and forever. For me, oh God, I pray that I will be more like Jesus tomorrow than I am today.

VERSE:

"Jesus Christ is the same yesterday and today and forever." (Hebrews 13:8)

QUOTATION:

"[Spirituality] is a mixed-up, topsy-turvy, helter-skelter godliness that turns our lives into an upside-down toboggan ride full of unexpected turns, surprise bumps, and bone-shattering crashes...a life ruined by a Jesus who loves us right into his arms."—Mike Yaconelli

TRUTH
(honesty, reality, fact, whole story, authentic)

EXPERIENCE:

Telling the truth requires courage.
When you tell the truth to others,
it makes it easier for them

to forgive you.

Write down something you've been
hiding from a friend...
and today
share it with that friend.

REFLECT:

In what ways might you be avoiding reality?

PRAYER:

Lord, give me the courage to experience what is on this page every day of my life.

VERSE:

"Therefore confess your sins to each other and pray for each other so that you may be healed. The prayer of a righteous person is powerful and effective."
(James 5:16)

QUOTATION:

"When in doubt, tell the truth."—Mark Twain

CLOTHING

EXPERIENCE:

Cut a small piece of fabric from one of your shirts or T-shirts and glue it here.

REFLECT:

What are your **favorite clothing stores?**

How many of your clothing items could you give to **others** in **need?**

PRAYER:

Lord, help me to develop a relentless heart for those in need that transforms every decision I make.

QUOTATION:

"Charity is a virtue of the heart, and not of the hands."—Joseph Addison

SHOES

EXPERIENCE:

Glue a shoelace on the word **empathy** below.

empathy

REFLECT:

Think about what it would be like to walk in the shoes of someone you don't know very well. How can you get to know and **understand** that person better?

PRAYER:

Lord, show me whose shoes I could walk in and teach me something new about empathy today.

VERSE:

"Carry each other's burdens, and in this way you will fulfill the law of Christ." (Galatians 6:2)

QUOTATION:

"Ah, the first step in humility: Listening."
—Dr. Michael Beckwith

TABLE

EXPERIENCE:

Look online for an **easy recipe**
            to make for your **friends**.
    Glue the recipe here as a **reminder**
            of your **fun dinner party**.

TABLE   83

REFLECT:

How did it feel cooking for your friends?
Will you continue
to serve more people
in other ways?

PRAYER:

Lord, help me to have an **open table** in my heart for others **at all times.**

VERSE:

"When evening came, **Jesus** was reclining at the table with **the Twelve.**" (Matthew 26:20)
Who are your "twelve"...and why?

QUOTATION:

"**The next best thing** to being wise oneself is to live in a circle of those who are."—C. S. Lewis

GARBAGE

EXPERIENCE:

Dig through some garbage
and find something of value.
Glue it and write about it here.

REFLECT:

Rediscover the **value** of something you once threw away.

PRAYER:

Lord, please help me to rediscover the parts of my life that only you can bring value to.

VERSE:

"Therefore, if anyone is in Christ, the new creation has come: The old has gone, the new is here!" (2 Corinthians 5:17)

QUOTATION:

"The gospel is absurd and the life of Jesus is meaningless unless we believe that He lived, died, and rose again with but one purpose in mind: to make brand-new creations."

—Brennan Manning

NOODLES

EXPERIENCE:

Using glue and cooked spaghetti noodles, spell out an attitude you would like to strengthen.

REFLECT:

How can you go about
        strengthening that attitude?

PRAYER:

Lord, you are my strength. Help me to apply that clarity to my life and extend it to others.

VERSE:

"But the fruit of the Spirit is love, joy, peace, forbearance, kindness, goodness, faithfulness, gentleness and self-control." (Galatians 5:22-23)

QUOTATION:

"Stay committed to your decisions, but stay flexible in your approach."—Tony Robbins

GLITTER

EXPERIENCE:

Using glitter and glue,
create words below that represent
what makes you come alive.

REFLECT:

How could you use these words to
light up the lives of others?

PRAYER:

Lord, may my life be a reflection of these words and help me encourage others to do the same.

VERSE:

"Let your light shine before others, that they may see your good deeds and glorify your Father in heaven." (Matthew 5:16)

QUOTATION:

"Has your relationship with God changed the way you live your life?"—Francis Chan

PUZZLE

EXPERIENCE:

Outline or draw a few puzzle pieces. Write down your faith questions in and around them.

REFLECT:

What people in your life can you approach to help you make sense of these questions?

How can these people help you complete your life puzzle?

PRAYER:

Lord, thank you that no question I have is out of bounds for you.

VERSE:

"Jesus answered, 'I am the way and the truth and the life. No one comes to the Father except through me.'" (John 14:6)

QUOTATION:

"The moment God is figured out with nice neat lines and definitions, we are no longer dealing with God."—Rob Bell

GRASS STAIN

EXPERIENCE:

Take a handful of grass
and rub it into this page.

REFLECT:

Grass stains typically happen **when people live carefree lives** full of **playfulness** and **laughter.** How much did you **thrive** when you **lived that way** during your **younger days?**

PRAYER:

Lord, show me daily what it means to live life in the fullness of who I was created to be.

VERSE:

"The thief comes only to steal and kill and destroy; I have come that they may have life, and have it to the full." (John 10:10)

QUOTATION:

"Your job is the relentless pursuit of who God has made you to be. And anything else you do is sin and you need to repent of it."
—Rob Bell

SHOE PRINT

EXPERIENCE:

Mark this page with your shoe print, as well as with the shoe print of a close friend.

REFLECT:

Consider how you learn to both lead and follow.

PRAYER:

Lord, give me the strength to live my life in a way that not only points people to you but also points me toward people who look like you.

VERSE:

"As iron sharpens iron, so one person sharpens another." (Proverbs 27:17)

QUOTATION:

"A leader is one who can lead as well as he can follow. These are two sides of the same coin."—anonymous

FINGER PRINT

EXPERIENCE:

Dip your fingers in **something messy** and fingerprint this page in an inspired way.

REFLECT:

Take some time to closely examine
        the patterns of your fingerprints
    and the details the lines make.

PRAYER:

Lord, thank you for always knowing every detail of my life even when I feel unsure or lost. Help me to trust you with the unique plan you have for me, for I know I am special.

VERSE:

"Before I formed you in the womb I knew you, before you were born I set you apart..." (Jeremiah 1:5)

QUOTATION:

"There is nothing worth living for, unless it is worth dying for."—Elisabeth Elliot

EXPERIENCE:

Make a collage
using old CDs and favorite lyrics.

REFLECT:

What does your favorite music tell you about yourself, past and present?

How can it evoke emotion or empower you to act in certain ways?

PRAYER:

Lord, allow me to hear your music of the world on a daily basis so that I may allow it to encourage me to love with all my heart.

VERSE:

"Being confident of this, that he who began a good work in you will carry it on to completion until the day of Christ Jesus." (Philippians 1:6)

QUOTATION:

"We are all hypocrites in transition. I am not who I want to be, but I am on the journey there, and thankfully I am not whom I used to be."—Erwin McManus

UPSIDE DOWN

EXPERIENCE:

With a pencil, turn your book
upside down and
write down as many of
your questions,
frustrations,
and doubts
about God that you can.
Then turn the book
right-side up
and write down as many
ways you delight in the Lord as you can.

REFLECT:

How can your questions about God
create a deeper relationship with God?
How can all the ways you
delight in the Lord
reflect upon your character?

PRAYER:

Lord, give me the peace that only you can give to celebrate you in the midst of my greatest doubts and trust you in my greatest joys.

VERSE:

Read Psalm 9 (David praises God); then read Psalm 10 (David questions God).

QUOTATION:

"Doubt isn't the opposite of faith; it is an element of faith."—Paul Tillich

RECYCLE

EXPERIENCE:

Glue a recycled piece of paper
to this page.
Write down in the page the areas in your life
that feel like trash
and need to be made into something new.

REFLECT:

How will you **change** the areas of your life that **need recycling?**

How will your **life change** because of that?

PRAYER:

Lord, you alone can take the areas of my life that look nothing like you and make them into something brand new. Please do so in my life right now.

VERSE:

"For I am convinced that neither death nor life, neither angels nor demons, neither the present nor the future, nor any powers, neither height nor depth, nor anything else in all creation, will be able to separate us from the love of God that is in Christ Jesus our Lord." (Romans 8:38-39)

QUOTATION:

"I only feel angry when I see waste. When I see people throwing away things that we could use."
—Mother Teresa

FORGIVE NESS

EXPERIENCE:

Tear off the top of this page
and write on the piece of paper a note
seeking forgiveness
from someone
you have wronged.
Below, write a note to someone
who has forgiven you.

REFLECT:

Is it easier to seek forgiveness or to forgive?

What is holding you back from seeking forgiveness from those you've wronged?

PRAYER:

Lord, help me live without pride so I can offer and seek unconditional forgiveness.

VERSE:

"Bear with each other and forgive one another if any of you has a grievance against someone. Forgive as the Lord forgave you." (Colossians 3:13)

QUOTATION:

"To forgive is to set a prisoner free and discover that the prisoner was you."
—Lewis B. Smedes

BUCKET LIST

EXPERIENCE:

Respond to the following with
big dreams
and complete honesty:

Before I die I hope to...

The following makes me feel most alive...

I hope I never,...

The following weighs me down,...

REFLECT:

who are the people in your life
who will help you
make these things a reality?

PRAYER:

Lord, please grant me the courage, strength, and creativity to live a full life for you.

VERSE:

"Taste and see that the LORD is good; blessed is the one who takes refuge in him." (Psalm 34:8)

QUOTATION:

"Why not go out on a limb? Isn't that where the fruit is?"—Frank Scully

TWO DOLLARS

EXPERIENCE:

Live on no more than two dollars for the entire day.

Write about your experience and how your mind was stretched.

REFLECT:

How can you help at least one person who's living on next to nothing?

PRAYER:

Lord, as I learn to **empathize with others**, help me consider what in my life **needs to change** so others can **share in my riches.**

VERSE:

"For the **poor will never cease** from the land; therefore I **command you**, saying, 'You shall **open your hand wide** to your brother, to **your poor** and **your needy**, in your land.'" (Deuteronomy 15:11, NKJV)

QUOTATION:

"If you can't feed **a hundred people**, then feed **just one.**"—Mother Teresa

REQUEST

EXPERIENCE:

Request advice from someone
very different than you
and write here about that advice.

REFLECT:

What did you learn from the advice that can help you grow into a stronger person? What other people (different than you) can speak into your life?

PRAYER:

Lord, show me your presence through people who are different than me.

VERSE:

"Finally, brothers and sisters, whatever is true, whatever is noble, whatever is right, whatever is pure, whatever is lovely, whatever is admirable—if anything is excellent and praiseworthy—think about such things." (Philippians 4:8)

QUOTATION:

"We must learn to live together as brothers or perish together as fools."
—Martin Luther King, Jr.

EXPERI ENCE

EXPERIENCE:

Make a list of 10 mistakes you've seen others make that you hope to never make.

REFLECT:

In what ways can you learn from others' mistakes and keep them from happening in your own life?

PRAYER:

Lord, help me to learn from others' mistakes without thinking that I'm immune to making them.

VERSE:

"No, dear brothers and sisters, I have not achieved it, but I focus on this one thing: Forgetting the past and looking forward to what lies ahead, I press on to reach the end of the race and receive the heavenly prize for which God, through Christ Jesus, is calling us."
(Philippians 3:13-14, NLT)

QUOTATION:

"Learn all you can from the mistakes of others. You won't have time to make them all yourself."
—Alfred Sheinwold

PROMISE

EXPERIENCE:

Make a **promise** to
a friend, a family member,
and to yourself
that will take you
out of your comfort zone.

REFLECT:

What were your thoughts
during this experience?
How hard will it be for you to work
to keep your promise?

PRAYER:

Lord, may the commitments I have shared become the actions that affect many future generations.

VERSE:

"Jesus looked at them and said, 'With man this is impossible, but with God all things are possible.'" (Matthew 19:26)

QUOTATION:

"I am always doing that which I can not do, in order that I may learn how to do it."—Pablo Picasso

MAKE A LIST

EXPERIENCE:

Make a list of all the ways in which
you have wished you could get even with someone.
Then cross out each item
and write how you would
want to be treated if the
situation were reversed.

REFLECT:

How can you gain the courage
to treat others the way you would
want to be treated?

PRAYER:

Lord, remind me of this truth that gets so easily twisted in my world.

VERSE:

"So in everything, do to others what you would have them do to you, for this sums up the Law and the Prophets." (Matthew 7:12)

QUOTATION:

"Experience is not what happens to a man; it is what a man does with what happens to him."
—Aldous Huxley

START A MOVEMENT

EXPERIENCE:

Have a **bold conversation with God** concerning his will for you and your life.
Take notes on what God might be saying to you and what God might be calling you to do for him.

REFLECT:

How does it make you feel that you have God's full attention for every request, small and large?

PRAYER:

Lord, show me the power found in a life of prayer as I seek after your will in my life.

VERSE:

"The prayer of a righteous person is powerful and effective." (James 5:16b)

"This is the confidence we have in approaching God: that if we ask anything according to his will, he hears us. And if we know that he hears us—whatever we ask—we know that we have what we asked of him." (1 John 5:14-15)

QUOTATION:

"Every great movement of God can be traced to a kneeling figure."—D. L. Moody

SILENT STRENGTH

EXPERIENCE:

Read the verse below and,
        without the use of words,
    express your reaction all over this page.

In the same way,
    the Spirit helps us
            in our weakness.
We do not know what we ought to pray for,
        but the Spirit himself
            intercedes for us
    through **wordless groans.**
        (Romans 8:26)

REFLECT:

What **weak areas** in your life
     may **God be working on**
          right now in ways that you can't describe?

PRAYER:

Lord, in the midst of my weakest hour may you be my greatest strength.

VERSE:

"In the same way, the Spirit helps us in our weakness. We do not know what we ought to pray for, but the Spirit himself intercedes for us through wordless groans." (Romans 8:26)

QUOTATION:

"Is prayer your steering wheel or your spare tire?"—Corrie Ten Boom

SPLATTER

EXPERIENCE:

Using bold colors,
splatter paint of different colors
all over the page
representing areas in your life
that make you nervous or scared.
After the paint dries, label each area accordingly.

REFLECT:

What are the **triggers** in your life
that cause you to **hold tightly**
to that which you should **give to God?**

PRAYER:

Lord, calm my anxious heart as I rest comfortably in the mystery of your love.

VERSE:

"Do not be anxious about anything, but in every situation, by prayer and petition, with thanksgiving, present your requests to God. And the peace of God, which transcends all understanding, will guard your hearts and your minds in Christ Jesus." (Philippians 4:6-7)

QUOTATION:

"I have been driven many times upon my knees by the overwhelming conviction that I had nowhere else to go."—Abraham Lincoln

PRAYER

EXPERIENCE:

Open your newspaper and find stories
that need and circumstances
prayer.

Cut out the headlines, glue them to the page,
and cry out to God
on behalf of those who need help
and healing today.

REFLECT:

What does it do to your heart
when you know that your prayers for people
you don't know somehow
make a difference?

PRAYER:

Lord, may I **never doubt your power** as I intercede on behalf of others.

VERSE:

"I urge, then, **first of all**, that petitions, prayers, intercession and thanksgiving be made **for all people**—for kings and all those in authority, that we may live peaceful and quiet lives in all godliness and **holiness.** This is good, and pleases God our Savior, who wants **all people to be saved** and to come to a **knowledge** of the **truth.**" (1 Timothy 2:1-4)

QUOTATION:

"Prayer does not fit us for the greater work; **prayer is the greater work.**"
—Oswald Chambers

HEADLINE

EXPERIENCE:

Write a newspaper article,
complete with a **headline**,
about what your life would look like
if God said yes to all your requests.

REFLECT:

How can you **protect yourself**
from the **selfish desires** of your heart?

PRAYER:

Lord, thank you for loving me enough to protect me from some of my prayers.

VERSE:

"Search me, God, and know my heart; test me and know my anxious thoughts. See if there is any offensive way in me, and lead me in the way everlasting." (Psalm 139:23-24)

QUOTATION:

"Some of God's greatest gifts are unanswered prayers."—Garth Brooks

SELF-WORTH

EXPERIENCE:

Using a pencil, make a list of all the reasons
why God should not love you.
Lightly erase the list and with a
permanent marker

write the text of Matthew 11:28-30
over the erased words as you
reflect on your life.

REFLECT:

what is holding you back from letting the words of this verse become the story of your life?

PRAYER:

Lord, thank you for **not giving up on me** even when I have given up on you.

VERSE:

"Are you tired? Worn out? Burned out on religion? Come to me. Get away with me and you'll recover your life. I'll show you how to take a **real rest.** Walk with me and work with me—watch how I do it. Learn the unforced rhythms of grace. I won't lay anything heavy or ill-fitting on you. Keep company with me and you'll learn to live freely and lightly." (Matthew 11:28-30, The Message)

QUOTATION:

"The grace of God is dangerous. It's lavish, excessive, outrageous, and scandalous. God's grace is ridiculously inclusive."—Mike Yaconelli

EXPERIENCE:

Take some cold water and make a list of
all the great uses for water in your life.
Now boil some water and make a list
of all its great uses in your life.
Then combine the cold and hot water
and make a list of the all the great uses
for lukewarm water in your life.

REFLECT:

What areas in your life are lukewarm and good for nothing?

PRAYER:

Lord, **transform** the lukewarm parts of my life into **useful** areas for you.

VERSE:

"I know your **deeds**, that you are neither **cold** nor **hot.** I wish you were either **one or the other!** So, because you are **lukewarm**—neither hot nor cold—I am about to **spit you out** of my mouth." (Revelation 3:15-16)

QUOTATION:

"Christianity is **no longer** life changing, **it is life enhancing.** Jesus doesn't change people into **wild-eyed radicals** anymore. He changes them into 'nice people.' If Christianity is simply about **being nice,** I'm not interested."—Mike Yaconelli

EXPERIENCE:

The grace of God gives us what we don't deserve. Take time to write a thank-you note to God about your weaknesses while thanking God for the grace he offers you every single day.

REFLECT:

What needs to change in your life
so you can **embrace** the grace of God
and model it for others?

PRAYER:

Lord, forgive me for the times when I live in opposition of you.

VERSE:

"But he said to me, 'My grace is sufficient for you, for my power is made perfect in weakness.' Therefore I will boast all the more gladly about my weaknesses, so that Christ's power may rest on me. That is why, for Christ's sake, I delight in weaknesses, in insults, in hardships, in persecutions, in difficulties. For when I am weak, then I am strong." (2 Corinthians 12:9-10)

QUOTATION:

"Apparently God doesn't care who He loves. He is not very careful about the people He calls His friends or the people He calls His church."
—Mike Yaconelli

HUMILITY

EXPERIENCE:

Use this page to write an **apology note**
to a person you were convinced was **wrong**
about an issue but now know was right.

Deliver the note today.

REFLECT:

Are you more concerned with being right than doing the right thing?

PRAYER:

Lord, please grant me the humility to admit when others are right and seek forgiveness when necessary.

VERSE:

"He guides the humble in what is right and teaches them his way." (Psalm 25:9)

"For those who exalt themselves will be humbled, and those who humble themselves will be exalted." (Matthew 23:12)

QUOTATION:

"People find it far easier to forgive others for being wrong than for being right."—J.K. Rowling

SHADOW

EXPERIENCE:

Trace a shadow of your hand
or any other object on this page.

REFLECT:

Do you feel as though you're living in the shadow
of someone else's life?

How can your strengths help you
stand out and create your own story?

PRAYER:

Lord, help me realize that I am special, and you planned my life from the very beginning.

VERSE:

"It's in Christ that we find out who we are and what we are living for. Long before we first heard of Christ and got our hopes up, he had his eye on us, had designs on us for glorious living, part of the overall purpose he is working out in everything and everyone."
(Ephesians 1:11-12, The Message)

QUOTATION:

"To live by grace means to acknowledge my whole life story, the light side and the dark. In admitting my shadow side I learn who I am and what God's grace means."—Brennan Manning